Baby Girl:
Welcome To Your Family

Sherry Ramrattan Smith and Matthew Brian Smith

AuthorHouse™
1663 Liberty Drive
Bloomington, IN 47403
www.authorhouse.com
Phone: 1-800-839-8640

Published by AuthorHouse 01/16/2012

ISBN: 978-1-4685-3754-3 (sc)

Library of Congress Control Number: 2011963721

This book is printed on acid-free paper.

authorHOUSE®

A Considerate Curriculum

Curriculum is about choices we make every day. A *Considerate Curriculum* encourages us to critically examine our actions and carefully consider how our interactions and relationships can be more supportive and nurturing.

Visit Sherry's website for additional resources, free lesson suggestions, and to read weekly blogs with ideas that can help in implementing a *considerate curriculum*. You can also book workshops with Sherry. Please contact her at:

By mail	A Time To Learn
	9-3151 Lakeshore Road
	Suite 437
	Kelowna, BC V1W 3S9
Website	www.atimetolearn.ca
Email	sherry@atimetolearn.ca

CPSIA information can be obtained
at www.ICGtesting.com
Printed in the USA
276609LV00001B

For Mila
Madyn's baby sister,
born January 3, 2012

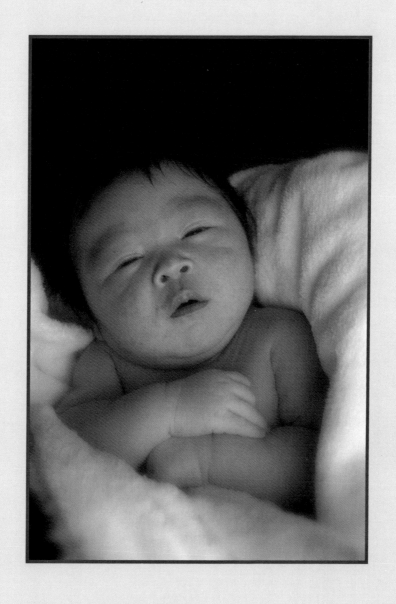

Meet Madyn Rosabelle. She is our beautiful granddaughter.

Dad takes one look at Madyn and falls in love with his gorgeous daughter.

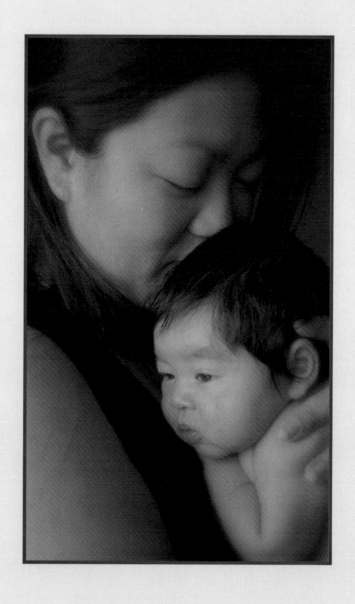

Mom cuddles Madyn and keeps her precious
little girl warm.

She feels safe and happy with her mom and dad.

Madyn enjoys bath time.

She plays with her yellow rubber duck.

She loves to spend time with Grandpa Meng and Grandma Vone.

Our families get together for a traditional
Buddhist blessing to celebrate Madyn's birth.

Grandma Sherry always has a big smile for
her granddaughter.

Grandpa Brian loves to hug her even when she is crying.

Madyn meets her uncles, Ben and Morris.

She also meets Great Grandmas, Noreen and
Rose, and Great Grandpa Jack.

Family and friends like to visit Madyn to see how she grows and changes.

Shiloh is Madyn's dog. She also likes to play with Sparky.

As soon as Madyn wakes up she is ready to play.

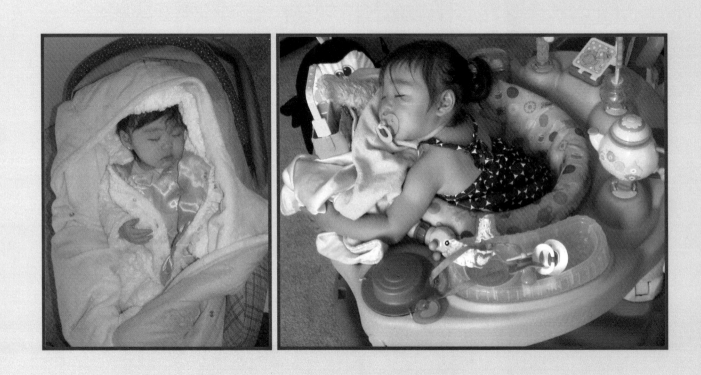

When she feels tired, she just takes a nap.

Madyn has her first swim in a big swimming pool. She likes the water.

As she grows up she continues to enjoy playing in the water.

Madyn learns to do lots of activities. She plays her piano and dances like a ballerina.

She sings songs, colours pictures, and rides her bike.

Madyn and her dad have lots of fun together.

Madyn helps her Great Grandma Rose to blow
out her birthday sparklers. They celebrate
being big girls.